FIREFIGHTING

Behind the Scenes

Maria Mudd Ruth

WITH PHOTOGRAPHS BY Scott Sroka

Houghton Mifflin Company

Boston 1998

For Mike, Will, and Nelson,
   my men behind the scenes.
      — M.M.R.

For my father,
   Edward Sroka, the first firefighter I ever knew.
      — S.S.

We respectfully thank the men and women who serve the fire departments in Washington, D.C.; Loudoun County and Fairfax County in Virginia; Montgomery County and Prince George's County in Maryland; and the cities of South Pasadena and Tampa in Florida. We are grateful to them for their contributions to this book and for their heroic service to their communities.

The text of this book is set in Adobe Garamond.
Book design by Susan Sherman, Ars Agassiz, Cambridge, Massachusetts

Library of Congress Cataloging-in-Publication Data

Mudd Ruth, Maria.
Firefighting: behind the scenes / by Maria Mudd Ruth with photographs by Scott Sroka.
p. cm.
Summary: Explains the challenging and dangerous work performed by firefighters, the clothing they wear, and the special gear they use.
ISBN 0-395-70129-5
1. Fire extinction—Juvenile literature.   [1. Firefighters. 2. Fire extinction.
3. Occupations.] I. Sroka, Scott, ill. II. Title.
TH9148.M76   1998
628.9'25—DC21   97-11233 CIP AC

Printed in Singapore
TWP 10 9 8 7 6 5 4 3 2 1

Contents

Firefighting Then and Now

Since the colonial days in America, firefighters have symbolized strength and courage in the communities they serve and protect. Modern-day firefighters (opposite) carry on centuries-old traditions of teamwork and dedication.

At five A.M. on a cold winter morning, a homeowner is awakened by the smell of smoke. Rushing downstairs, he sees his living room in flames. Panicked, he runs upstairs, calling to his sleeping wife and children to wake up and get out of the house. In their pajamas and bathrobes they rush out of the house through the back door. The man bangs desperately on a neighbor's door, shouting to be let in. His wife is trying to comfort their crying children. The neighbor opens the door, and the family rushes in out of the cold. The man runs to the phone and calls 911. He speaks quickly and for only a few seconds. He rejoins his family to watch his house from the neighbor's front door. The windows are glowing orange; smoke is wafting out of the open back door and billowing out of the chimney. In less than a minute, the family hears wailing sirens and low, rumbling horns. As the first fire engine comes into view, its flashing red and white lights brighten the dark street. Seconds later, more fire trucks, a rescue squad, and an ambulance appear on the scene. The father rushes out to the trucks. Their house is quickly surrounded by a dozen firefighters. They move hoses, ladders, axes, and chain saws off the trucks into position around the house, cut the roof open, smash the windows, and release powerful streams of water onto the fire. Clouds of smoke and steam rise into the sky. They wait, watching their house, wondering if they will lose everything in this nightmare.

Early firefighting "trucks" ranged from simple horse-drawn wagons pumped by teams of firefighters to ornate engines powered by steam, as shown here.

Courtesy, Rensselaer County Historical Society, Troy, New York

The family has seen fires like this on television and in newspapers. They have watched news reports showing dramatic pictures of firefighters in action at burning buildings. The family knows the firefighters are doing their job, but they don't really understand what is going on in the chaos of trucks, flashing lights, ladders, and hoses surrounding their home. Who is in charge? How do they know what to do first? Why do the firefighters chop a hole in the roof? The news reports don't explain who these firefighters are and why they would want a job that puts them in constant danger.

There are more than one million firefighters in the United States. Daily, they risk their lives to save people and protect property. It takes strength and courage to put on eighty pounds of protective clothing and equipment, and carry heavy tools and hose lines into buildings that are hotter than 1,200 degrees Fahrenheit. These buildings are so smoky that firefighters often cannot see their own feet. To stay below the level of heat and smoke they have to crawl on their hands and knees or slide along on their stomachs. They cannot hear one another because protective hoods and helmets cover their ears and plastic facepieces muffle their voices. To communicate, they must press their facepieces together and shout. If they become separated from one another, run out of air, or are lost, they must search for a hose and follow it out of the building before they are overcome by smoke.

In spite of the danger and the hard work, most fire departments have long waiting lists of men and women who want to join. These modern firefighters are part of a long history of organized firefighting that in America dates back to colonial days.

Fires were a serious problem for the early settlers. Their wooden houses had thatch roofs and burned very easily. Even the chimneys of their fireplaces were sometimes made of wood. When a fire broke out, villagers sounded the alarm by running through the streets shouting "Fire!" or by beating drums

Tremendous horsepower and manpower were needed to handle the heavy and often cumbersome nineteenth-century steam engines.

Courtesy, Fire Apparatus Journal Collection, MAND Library, NYC Fire Academy, Randall's Island, New York

or ringing the bells of churches and meetinghouses. Everyone who heard the alarm rushed to the scene of the fire to join a "bucket brigade." The men would form a line from a pond, stream, well, or cistern to the fire, and pass buckets of water to throw on the fire. Women and children would form another line and pass the empty buckets back to the water supply. This was a slow way to put out a fire.

New York City, then called New Amsterdam, established the colonies' first fire prevention system in 1647. Fire wardens inspected houses and chimneys for fire hazards. Homeowners paid fines for having dirty chimneys, and the money was used to buy ladders, buckets, and hooks for pulling off burning thatch. A team of eight men, called a rattle watch, patrolled the streets at night to watch for fires. When a fire was discovered, they shook wooden rattles to alert townspeople to the danger and to call for help. In

Modern gasoline-powered fire engines, introduced in the early 1900s, replaced both the steam engine and the horses.

1736 Benjamin Franklin founded the colonies' first volunteer fire company, in Philadelphia. Other volunteer fire companies were soon organized in other colonies. George Washington, John Hancock, Alexander Hamilton, Samuel Adams, and Paul Revere all served as volunteers. People began to see firefighters as heroes who would drop whatever they were doing and rush to the fire as soon as the alarm sounded.

The first engines for pumping water onto fires were brought from England to New York in the 1730s. The "engine" was actually a pump mounted on a rectangular box or tub on wheels. It was pulled by men to the

fire. The bucket brigade poured water into the tub while a team of men worked the pump like a seesaw to produce water pressure. Teams of forty to sixty men were needed to haul and operate some models. As these engines became more powerful, horses were introduced to pull the heavy engines to the fire.

Steam-powered engines were invented in 1819, and fire departments began using them to pump water. Some of the early steam engines weighed more than 20,000 pounds, and were difficult for even a team of horses to pull. Firefighters soon discovered that horses would run faster if a dog led the way. Many breeds were used, but Dalmations were the best. Dalmations still live at many fire stations. No longer needed to lead horses, they are watch-dogs, companions, and reminders of firefighting history. In the early 1900s, gasoline-powered engines replaced the steamers and the horses. These pow-erful engines ushered in a new era of firefighting.

As fire engines were changing, so were the fire departments. During the days of hand-powered engines, hundreds of volunteers from several fire

Fire stations come in many shapes and sizes: older city stations (top left and right) were first built to house horses. Later they became homes for a few trucks and enough firefighters to serve a neighborhood. Newer and larger suburban stations (bottom) are equipped to serve several towns.

Four garage doors topped by a row of windows provide clues to passersby that this station holds at least four vehicles and several upstairs bedrooms for on-duty fire-fighters.

departments might be needed to fight a fire. In some towns and cities, the traditional rivalry between departments racing to the fire became intense. Buildings would be left to burn as the volunteers fought with each other to be the first to put water on the fire. When steam engines came in, fewer firefighters were needed to handle the equipment. Many fire departments dismissed their rowdy volunteers and hired paid employees. In 1853, Cincinnati, Ohio, became the first city with a fully paid fire department. Regular firefighters were paid sixty dollars a year to report to fires when needed.

The first fire stations were small wooden sheds where a community kept its buckets, ladders, and hooks. Over the years, stations grew larger to accommodate horses, steam pumpers, motorized engines, and firefighters who slept at the station. Depending on when and where they were built, fire

Camaraderie is an important part of every fire department, whether the fire-fighters are on duty at their station, or working on the scene of a fire, or relaxing after training exercises.

stations may be as simple as an extra-large garage or as grand as a fancy brick church, with tall steeples, balconies, and bell towers. In many cities, tall, narrow fire stations are sandwiched between other buildings. Today fire stations may include not only a large garage for trucks and equipment, but also equipment repair rooms, a kitchen, exercise and recreation rooms, a laundry room, sleeping quarters, meeting rooms, and offices.

Today firefighters work either as paid career professionals or as volunteers. A fire station may be all volunteer, all career, or some of each. Career firefighters work regular shifts, usually twenty-four hours on duty, then forty-eight hours off. In big cities there may be as many as fifteen firefighters on duty at one time. During their shifts they live at the fire station. Their sleep and meals can be interrupted at any time by a fire alarm. At a busy station they might get out of bed five or six times in a night to answer calls.

In the United States, three out of four firefighters are volunteers. They may be high school or college students, retired professional firefighters, or people whose paying jobs allow them to rush to a fire when necessary. Busy volunteer stations are staffed in shifts like the professional stations, and sometimes a small group of paid firefighters works day shifts during the week. Less busy stations may have just one person on duty or be completely unmanned. At these stations the volunteers are on call twenty-four hours a day, seven days a week, although they do not have to answer every call. When their pagers sound, firefighters who can reach the station within five minutes drop everything and hurry there, hoping to arrive in time to gear up and get a seat. Latecomers who "don't make the truck" are disappointed as they watch the trucks pull out of the station without them. If not enough firefighters arrive in time, the dispatcher must signal a nearby station.

Volunteer fire departments in small towns may be as simple as a garage for storing trucks and equipment.

Becoming a Firefighter

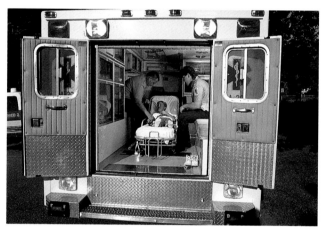

Firefighters are highly skilled men and women who perform many jobs in addition to fighting fires (top). Many firefighters are trained as emergency medical workers (bottom).

Firefighters do many jobs. They may be called to the scene of automobile accidents, forest fires, airplane crashes, explosions, collapsed buildings, and medical emergencies. They rescue people during tornadoes, hurricanes, and floods, and they help clean up afterward. They sometimes have to deliver babies. At some stations, more than half of the calls are medical emergencies rather than fires.

Within a fire department, there are different kinds of jobs. Fire and arson investigators try to discover how a fire started. Fire prevention officers inspect schools, movie theaters, stores, and other public buildings to look for fire hazards. Training officers teach classes about fires and how to fight them. Lots of ordinary jobs also have to be done in a fire station, such as ordering new equipment and uniforms, paying bills, organizing fund raisers, and answering nonemergency telephone calls. The firefighters have to shop, cook, clean the station, and make their beds.

To become a firefighter, a man or woman must be at least sixteen years old. In a volunteer department, applicants must meet certain basic qualifications before they are accepted into a training program. In paid departments, they must also pass written and physical tests. Students in a training program learn about building construction so they will be able to guess how a fire will

During their training courses, students practice using their equipment and extinguishing fires at a nearby indestructible "burn building."

move through the walls and rooms of a structure. They study the uses of various tools, ways to rescue people from buildings and cars, and emergency first aid. They learn the right way to wear their protective clothing, called turnout gear. They also learn how to wear and use the air tank, facepiece, and regulator of the self-contained breathing apparatus, or SCBA, which protects the firefighter's face and lungs from poisonous gases and smoke.

Wearing turnout gear, students set up and climb ladders, hook up hoses, rescue dummy "victims," cut holes in roofs, and use ventilating fans and other tools. Most fire departments have a building they can set on fire over and over again so students can practice fighting real fires. Some "burn buildings" are made of cinder block and concrete and are built to look like a house

on the front, apartment buildings on the sides, and a warehouse on the back. A department might create a smoke maze by connecting several trailers and filling them with the nonpoisonous "smoke" used for special effects in movies. Crawling on hands and knees, with SCBAs on their backs, students must feel their way out of the maze.

Most people enroll in firefighting school to become firefighters, but some have other reasons. Alicia Westman, a rural Virginia emergency medical technician, or EMT, went to firefighting school so that she would better understand how to treat the medical problems that firefighters suffer while battling a fire. After one especially stressful training exercise in a burn building, she herself experienced a high pulse rate, high blood pressure, and a terrible feeling of panic. "I'm forty-nine years old," Alicia says. "I have five kids. My kids and my husband think I'm crazy. I think they're right. This work is crazy. But at least I now know what these people go through fighting fires."

A few students in each class discover that they cannot be firefighters. When some people first put on an SCBA and enter a smoke-filled building, they run outside and rip off their masks, terrified. Others panic when they have to climb a four-story ladder. Some may become too upset when they see badly injured victims. Students must overcome these kinds of fears in order to become firefighters.

For other people, firefighting training is thrilling. They may be afraid at times, but they are excited by the experiences, just as they might be by mountain climbing or parachute jumping. One firefighter says, "We might try to deny it, but we like the danger. But that's only part of it. It shouldn't be the main reason you become a firefighter. If it is, you're going to be dangerous. You're going to take stupid risks."

The importance of teamwork is emphasized in training. For many people, teamwork is a new experience. They have to learn to take orders from

Experienced firefighters and instructors teach students to operate the pumper truck (top), carry hoses in and out of fires (bottom), and work in dark and smoke-filled buildings (opposite).

Firefighting school includes many hours of classroom instruction, book learning, and training videos.

Students must learn the proper ways to carry and use ladders and other equipment.

officers. They also have to depend on others and know that others are depending on them. Some students freeze up because they are afraid they will make a mistake that results in an injury.

At the end of their classroom training, students take written, practical, oral, or physical tests. Even after they have passed their tests, firefighters continue to take classes. They have to learn how to handle fires or spills of the newest chemicals and pesticides and to use new firefighting equipment. Some may decide to become instructors, arson investigators, or airport firefighters. Colleges and universities that have fire science departments provide advanced degrees in firefighting, fire investigation, or fire department management. After many years of training and experience, a firefighter may be promoted to company officer, captain, lieutenant, then chief.

During their training (or afterward in a paid department), students work as probationary members—called probies or rookies—at the fire station where they will serve. Rookies learn how their station and its equipment work. They learn how to load fire hoses and the rules for responding to an alarm. They become familiar with the area, studying the roads and the locations of fire hydrants or other water supplies. They find out what kinds of buildings they may have to work in, such as houses, stores, factories, or barns. And they continue to learn about working as part of a team. During their probationary period, rookies go on fire calls with their company, but many departments do not allow them to go inside a burning building.

Firefighting Companies

Modern fire departments are made up of engines, often called pumper trucks, and ladder trucks. The engine and its crew are the engine company. The ladder truck and its crew are the ladder company. Each company includes three to six firefighters with at least one person—a sergeant, lieutenant, assistant chief, or chief—who acts as a supervisor.

The main job of the engine company is to get water to a fire, so each engine is equipped with a tank that holds as much as 1,000 gallons of water, hundreds of feet of hose, different types of nozzles, portable fire extinguish-

Firefighting companies take great pride in their jobs.

Pumper Control Panel

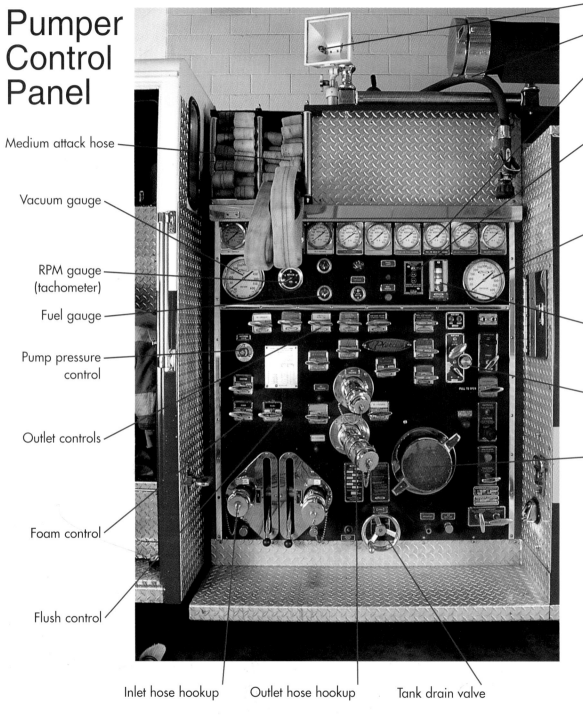

Floodlight

Light attack hose

Outlet gauges

Pump overheat light

Medium attack hose

Vacuum gauge

Pressure gauge

RPM gauge (tachometer)

Fuel gauge

Water level indicator

Pump pressure control

Outlet controls

Pressure relief valve control

Foam control

Fire hydrant inlet hose hookup

Flush control

Inlet hose hookup

Outlet hose hookup

Tank drain valve

ers, hydrant wrenches, and forcible-entry tools, such as crowbars and axes. A panel of controls and gauges on the engine helps firefighters adjust water pressure in each hose. In areas where medical emergencies greatly outnumber fires, the engine doubles as an emergency medical vehicle. It is equipped with stretchers, blankets, splints, bandages, ointments for treating burns, cold packs for sprains, and even kits for treating animal bites.

Ladder companies operate ladders to gain access to a fire. Ladders are made of metal or fiberglass. The ladder most often used is the aerial ladder, made up of several connected sections, which can extend up to 100 feet. Other ladders on the truck might be roof ladders and extension ladders. Ladder companies also search for and rescue victims and "open up" buildings with axes and saws to let out smoke. They search the building again after the main fire is out, looking for embers or anything else that could cause the fire to reignite.

Ladder trucks carry ladders that can be extended, folded, or inserted into a window from outside a building.

A well-equipped rescue vehicle (right) is essential in departments near major highways where automobile accidents occur frequently. Amphibious vehicles (opposite, top) can drive on land too swampy for a truck and in water too shallow for a boat. Fireboats (opposite, middle), which draw water directly from a lake, bay, or river, are stationed near docks of large port cities. Airport fire-crash trucks (opposite, bottom) equipped with special extinguishing foam are part of airport fire departments.

Many fire stations also have rescue and ambulance companies. The rescue firefighters are also highly trained medical workers who are EMTs, medics, or paramedics. They rescue people from burning or collapsed buildings, crushed automobiles, elevator shafts, water, and other dangers, and provide life-supporting medical care to victims until an ambulance can transport them to the hospital. The rescue vehicles are sometimes called "toolboxes on wheels" because they carry so much special equipment, such as axes, crowbars, chain saws, powerful ventilating fans, ropes, the Jaws of Life (a tool used to get into a car when the doors are too damaged to open), stretchers, medical supplies, extra SCBA tanks, fire extinguishers, and flashlights, as well as a variety of ladders. Some vehicles even carry a fifty-foot-high light tower that can light an area the size of a football field for nighttime rescues.

Many fire departments have other specialty vehicles. Cities on the water have fireboats to protect the docks, piers, and boats in the harbor. Departments in forested or mountainous areas have four-wheel-drive Jeeps that can travel on narrow dirt roads. Departments near airports and interstate highways have companies trained and equipped to handle fires or accidents involving hazardous materials such as gasoline.

When they first join a department, firefighters are usually assigned by the chief to either the ladder company or the engine company. In smaller departments, each person must be able to do both jobs. Most firefighters are also trained to be paramedics, EMTs, or rescue specialists. Some prefer one company over the other. Engineers say that what you need when running into a fire is water and that the real job of the firefighter is putting the "wet stuff on the hot stuff." Ladder company members say they can move faster with tools than with hoses, and they "aren't just standing around supporting a nozzle." And, they say, the engineers have all those dirty hoses to clean up at the end of a fire. Ladder companies just have their tools. Even though they have different jobs, the two companies work together as a team. Once the alarm goes off, personal feelings do not matter. No firefighter will stand around if the other company needs help.

Rivalry between companies, or between rookies and experienced firefighters, usually takes the form of teasing and practical jokes—lots of jokes. Firefighters may strap a member of the other company to a rescue backboard and stand him in the corner of the garage, have water fights, or spray the other company's vehicle with perfume. For rookies, the practical jokes are part of becoming one of the gang. "If they ignore you and leave you alone, they don't like you. If they mess with you, you're in," explains Captain Mike Lamb, a firefighter with thirteen years of experience.

Firefighting often runs through many generations of a family. John Wisner has been a firefighter for twenty-four years, and his father and grand-

Firefighters stay close together as they prepare to face the fire. To avoid getting disoriented or lost in dark, smoky buildings, they keep one hand on the boot of the firefighter in front of them and one hand on the charged hose line beside. In some cases, firefighters can see only the reflective trim on one another's gear.

father were firefighters before him. "I remember when I was growing up," John says, "I'd rush right out the door behind my father when he left the house on a call. No one could stop me." Many firefighters marry paramedics, EMTs, or other firefighters. One ambulance driver whose husband is a firefighter says, "It helps to have someone to talk to at home who really understands the stress and strain of this kind of work."

Robin and Bob Dryden are both volunteers at Company 2 in Loudoun County, Virginia. Robin grew up nearby, the daughter of the man who established the Blue Ridge Volunteer Fire and Rescue Station. Robin's mother organized the ladies' auxiliary, the volunteer organization that serves food and drinks to firefighters at the fire scene. Robin spent her free time at her father's station, cleaning trucks and equipment. At sixteen she enrolled in the Loudoun County Fire Training School. "There was never any pressure from my parents to become a firefighter. I was always interested in firefighting. I never want to see people suffer or get hurt. This is the way I can help."

Robin married Bob, a firefighter with the Blue Ridge station, and they moved to a house near the Company 2 station. Like many volunteers, Robin juggles two part-time jobs with her firefighting responsibilities. She also goes to school. Since she is not near the station during the day, she answers calls at night, between 9:30 P.M., when she goes to bed, and 5:00 A.M., when she leaves for work. Bob works near the station, so he usually answers calls during the day. Robin and Bob spend Monday nights at the station, training and practicing drills with the other volunteers. Sometimes they go on calls together. "When a call comes in at three A.M., it's much easier to get up and get dressed if we both go," she says.

Robin is among the growing number of women firefighters across the country. The first woman in the United States to become a full-time paid firefighter did so in 1976. Many male firefighters were concerned that women wouldn't be brave enough or strong enough to do the job. In some places, the all-male departments didn't want to change. Now, although more women want to do this work, it is still a struggle. Some women report that as rookies they were teased or treated rudely by the men, who hoped they would quit. The women had to prove that they were strong and committed before they were accepted as equals.

Since the 1970s, more and more women have become firefighters.

Firefighters are often in danger. While being too scared can get in the way of their job, a little fear often makes them more cautious and helps prevent them from getting hurt. Many rookies have "near misses," when their inexperience causes them to take unnecessary risks.

"Your adrenaline level changes as you go down the road on a call," says one engine driver. "By the time you get to a fire, you're really hyped up. Once you're there, your actions become automatic. Sometimes you don't even notice you're nervous or scared. You just do your job and don't think about it."

Sometimes, despite their hard work, firefighters see property destroyed and people injured or even killed. Usually they are able to recover quickly from such tragedies, but a time may come when one fire or accident is so terrible that they are too upset to go out on the next call. Thad Golas, who has served the fire station at the San Francisco International Airport for thirty years, remembers one of these: "The worst for me was when a Learjet blew up in front of the firehouse. I saw the plane take off. It got no more than five hundred feet up. I heard funny sounds, then I watched it explode. We got there in about twenty seconds, but there was nothing left of the aircraft. There we were, ready to help, but there was nothing we could do. It was such a helpless feeling."

Firefighters learn that the hardest order they have to give or follow is to let someone die rather than risk additional lives. Older firefighters remember the days when they were supposed to be tough guys who never needed help. Now each fire station has a peer counselor—a firefighter trained to talk with those who are seriously troubled or depressed by what they have seen. Sometimes a professional counselor is called in. Almost always, firefighters are able to go on with their work—but most will admit that some experiences will haunt them forever.

Responding to an Emergency

Calling 911 (above) is the quickest way to report a fire. This telephone number connects the caller to the nearest emergency communications center (left) where dispatchers are on duty twenty-four hours a day to send fire and rescue companies where there are needed.

When a fire is reported to 911, the caller is connected to a dispatcher in the area's emergency communications center. Each dispatcher sits in front of a computer screen, with two-way radios, microphones, maps, and telephones. Dispatchers must be qualified firefighters and EMTs. Before they can answer calls by themselves, they undergo six months of on-the-job training and are then supervised for a year. They learn to remain calm and to ask

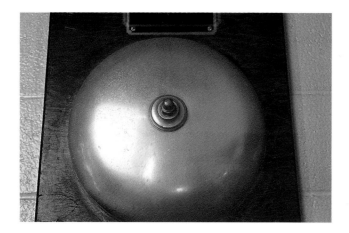

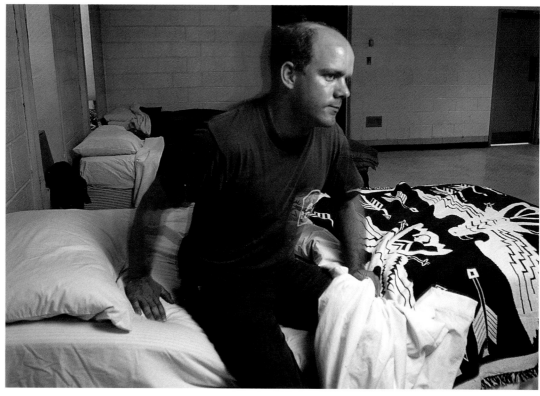

As soon as the dispatcher triggers the alarm bell inside the station (above) firefighters respond instantly. Every second counts in a fire emergency so firefighters sleep in their clothes (right).

the right questions. If the dispatcher sounds panicky, the person reporting the emergency may panic too and be unable to give the information needed.

Dispatching can be a tiring and difficult job. "Sometimes you'll have two or three hours without a single call," says one dispatcher. "Then all of a sudden the calls start coming in and you feel like you've worked a full day in about forty-five minutes. After one of these mornings I just had to get up and walk away and let the other guys handle the phones for a while."

When the dispatcher takes a fire call, his computer screen shows the kind of building, what the building is made of, the street address, cross street, phone number, and name of the owner of the house the person is calling from. If he is calling from his own house, the dispatcher will tell him to hang up, get himself and his family out, and call back from a neighbor's house. As

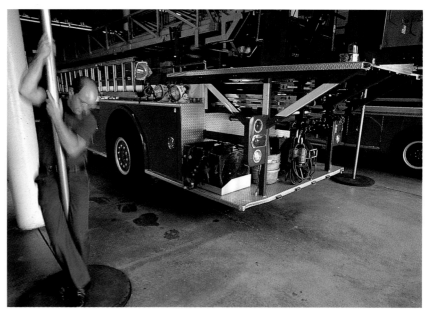

the caller describes the fire, the dispatcher types information into his computer: the type of emergency, what is burning, whether smoke and fire are visible from the outside, whether anyone is still in the house, the caller's name, and the exact location of the burning house.

The dispatcher's computer screen flashes the codes for the fire companies that have to be alerted. With a click of the mouse button, the computer rings the alarm inside the fire station closest to the incident, sets off the pagers of the volunteer firefighters, and sounds the station's siren. Then the dispatcher announces the information over the radio to the station and calls the necessary vehicles. Finally the dispatcher transmits the information to the fire station's computer printer. The firefighters who leave the station first will take the printout with them.

As soon as the dispatcher sets the alarm off in the station, the firefighters stop what they are doing and begin moving fast. They slide down the pole or run down the stairs to the garage and put on their turnout gear.

Sliding poles save time getting firefighters from the upstairs dormitory to their trucks parked in the garage below.

Firefighters put on their protective gear over their clothes. First their boots and turnout pants, then coat, protective hood, and helmet. They put on their air tank, face mask, and gloves in the trucks or at the scene of the fire.

First to go on are their turnout pants. To save time when dressing, firefighters leave their boots tucked into the legs of their turnout pants and the pants turned out over the boots. That way, they can climb into their boots and pants at the same time. The boots, which have steel plates inside to protect the firefighters' feet from nails or broken glass, are made of fire-resistant rubber and have nonskid treads.

Next comes the thigh-length coat, which closes with snaps and buckles. The coat and pants are made of three layers of material. The outer layer helps protect against temperatures over 1,200 degrees Fahrenheit. The next layer is a moisture barrier, for if water from a hose soaks through to the skin and then heats up, it can turn to steam and cause serious burns. The coat's inner, "thermal" layer is made of special synthetic fibers that trap air near the firefighter's body. That trapped air helps cool the heat coming in through the turnout gear. When close to a fire, firefighters have to remember to move their bodies constantly inside their turnout gear, keeping their coat and

Helmets have wide brims and padding on the inside. Helmets and fire-resistant hoods (not shown) protect the firefighters' heads from falling objects, burning embers, and scalding water.

Coats have high collars and large pockets for carrying several pounds of tools.

SCBA is a self-contained breathing apparatus. It includes a twenty-five-pound metal tank of breathing air and a plastic face shield with a breathing regulator.

Axes are used to break through walls, ceilings, doors, and windows to get to people trapped in a building and to let out smoke and dangerous gases.

Gloves are made of leather and special fire-resistant materials. They must be thick, strong, and flexible, but not bulky. Bulky gloves would make it difficult for the firefighters to handle small tools.

Pants often have heavy-duty suspenders so they won't sag when they get wet.

Boots are made of fire-resistant rubber and have steel plates inside to protect the firefighters' feet. They have nonskid treads to prevent slipping on wet surfaces.

Front-seat computers display directions to the fire scene as well as the dispatchers' updates about the fire. This information helps the firefighters plan their attack as soon as they board their truck (right) and while en route to the fire.

pants loose so the air can protect their skin. Firefighters get steam burns most often on their shoulders, where the SCBA straps press the coat against their skin. Underneath their turnout gear, firefighters wear pants and shirts, either their own clothes or, at some stations, a uniform.

Before climbing onto the trucks, the firefighters grab their hoods and helmets to put on as they ride. The helmets, made of hardened leather, plastic, or fiberglass, have earflaps, and are padded inside. The heat-resistant hoods cover their hair, ears, and neck. The firefighters will not put their gloves on until they reach the scene of the fire.

All of this special clothing cannot stop burns entirely. Most firefighters have had burning embers or scalding water get under their clothes or have had their hands burned through their gloves. Some fires are so hot that they burn right through all the layers of clothing.

When fully dressed, each firefighter wears about sixty pounds of gear, including a twenty-pound SCBA tank, which holds about thirty minutes' worth of compressed air. If firefighters are working unusually hard or are frightened, they breathe fast and can use up the air in less than ten minutes. Rookies tend to run out of air more quickly than experienced firefighters. When the air supply is low, a whistle or other noise warns the firefighter that there is about five minutes of air left. That allows time to get out of the building and refill the tank or get a new one. All air tanks also have another alarm. If a firefighter is injured or trapped and does not move for a minute or two, the alarm alerts firefighters outside the building that someone is in trouble.

In most companies, an engine is the first vehicle out of the station so that firefighters can connect hose lines to the pumper and the hydrant and have the hoses charged, or full of water, as soon as possible. The engine officer takes the computer printout from the fire station's communications room, and in less than a minute after the alarm sounds, the first engine pulls out of the station with four firefighters aboard. The officer radios the dispatcher, telling him that his company is responding to the fire.

Less than five minutes after that, a dozen or more volunteers arrive at the station. They put on their turnout gear and board the other two engines, the ladder truck, rescue vehicle, and ambulance along with the paid firefighters. Each truck usually has an officer on board. In some stations, the firefighters' seats on the engine or truck determine which jobs they will have at the fire scene. For instance, the engine driver operates the gauges and valves that control the flow of water to the hoses during the fire. The officer in the front passenger seat helps the driver navigate to the fire and operates the radio, to communicate with the dispatcher and other trucks.

As each vehicle pulls out of the garage, the driver turns on the sirens,

Information from the dispatcher can also be printed out on the fire station's computer and carried on board. Dispatchers can contact firefighters using their electronic belt pagers.

horns, flashing headlights, revolving lights, and strobe lights to warn motorists to move out of the way. The trucks speed down roads and through red lights. If traffic is heavy, a fire truck will even drive on the wrong side of the road. But most drivers exceed the speed limit by only about ten miles per hour. They want to get to the fire quickly but safely.

As they travel toward the fire scene, firefighters in the back of the trucks strap on their helmets and the SCBA tanks that are mounted on the back of each seat. The officer of the first engine becomes the incident commander, in charge of planning the "fire attack" and coordinating the actions of all the firefighters. At the fire, the incident commander takes a position near the engine so he can communicate on the two-way radio and have a clear view of most of the firefighters. The incident commander's job begins on the way to the fire when he makes an initial "size-up," or evaluation, of the fire. He reviews the information received from the dispatcher: How might the wind affect the way the fire behaves? Is the neighborhood densely populated? Where are the fire hydrants? How close is the building to other buildings? What may be burning inside? This size-up is critical in planning the best way to position vehicles, rescue victims, and put out the fire. The noise of the sirens and horns makes it necessary for the crew to wear earmuffs to protect their hearing. Inside the earmuffs is an intercom that allows the crew to communicate without shouting. The incident commander explains the size-up to the other firefighters and gives them instructions.

On the way to the fire scene, firefighters often share their knowledge of the house and neighborhood and prepare to "meet the bear." Firefighters often think of the fire as a living wild creature that they must learn to understand and respect before they can control it. They call fire "the bear," "the beast," "the animal," or "the orange man."

On the Scene

Firefighters work quickly to get water into the hose lines. While one firefighter opens the hydrant to hook up the pumper's supply hose, another awaits the signal to charge the attack lines.

Every fire is different, and every fire department's response to the fire will be different, too. Career firefighters at a big-city fire station using state-of-the-art equipment will handle a fire emergency one way, and a small station served by volunteers using older pumpers and trucks will handle it another way. The following scenario describes just one possible response to

a "room and contents" house fire in which one room and most everything in it is in flames. The two-story detached house is located in a suburban area. The fire station responding to the call is served by a combination of paid and volunteer firefighters. The dispatcher has requested at least three engines, a ladder truck, a rescue squad, and an ambulance.

Battling a major fire often requires several fire companies, many kinds of ladders, and a network of hose lines that supplies more than a thousand gallons of water a minute.

The pump operator keeps the pressure in the hose lines strong and constant during the fire attack.

Water from the pumper blasts out under great pressure. It takes several firefighters to hold and aim large attack lines.

As the first engine approaches the burning building, the incident commander informs the dispatcher that the engine is "on location" and reports the degree of visible smoke and fire.

The other vehicles arrive within seconds and are positioned around the house near fire hydrants and the entrances to the building. As the firefighters begin working, the incident commander gets out to talk to the homeowner or other witnesses and to make another size-up of the fire and the condition of the building. Now he has more detailed information about where people might be inside and where and how the fire may have started. He radios instructions to the company officers, then again radios the dispatcher with a report.

In a house fire, most of the critical work takes place in the first fifteen minutes after the trucks arrive. Firefighters work very rapidly and perform their assignments simultaneously or within seconds of each other. At this fire the most important job is to rescue any people still inside.

It would be too dangerous for the rescue team to enter the house without a charged hose line, since no one can tell if the fire has spread from the living room to other parts of the house. The engine company must first charge hose lines for the rescue team and also charge lines for the ladder company, which must ventilate the roof before the fire can be sprayed with water. Without proper ventilation, the smoke, steam, and heat produced when the water hits the fire would build up inside the house and make it too dangerous for firefighters to enter.

The first engine unloads two "attack lines" (hoses 1¼ to 2½ inches in diameter) and stretches them to the front of the house. The third engine stretches two attack lines to the back of the house. The pump operator, usually the driver, stays with the truck during the fire attack and adjusts the pump that controls the water pressure. Too little pressure may mean the water will not reach the fire. Too much pressure and the firefighters may not be able to control the hose, and the powerful streams of water could damage the building.

In cities and suburbs, the water needed to extinguish fires comes from fire hydrants, which are connected to underground pipes drawing water from a reservoir or water tower. In some places the color of the hydrant indicates how many gallons of water will flow out of it each minute: red hydrants produce less than 500 gallons a minute; light blue ones produce 1,500 gallons or more. In rural areas without hydrants, water is drawn from streams, rivers, ponds, or swimming pools to supplement the supply in the engines' 1,000-gallon tanks. If the water supply gets low, the pump operators tell the incident commander, who tells the dispatcher to send additional engines from other stations.

Most building fires are extinguished with water, but fires or spills involving dangerous materials such as gasoline, fuel oil, or pesticides are only made worse if water is added. These fires are controlled with special foam that blankets the burning material, cutting off the fire's air supply. Foam trucks are standard equipment at fire stations near airports, industrial sites, and major highways, where fires and other emergencies involving dangerous chemicals are most likely to occur.

Rescue company firefighters pick up one of the attack lines as four ladder company firefighters pick up the other. The pump operator at the third engine watches them, waiting for the hand signal that means "charge the line." The firefighters brace themselves. Within fifteen seconds, the flat attack line fills with water and becomes heavy and as hard as a steel bar. The power of these hoses is tremendous. Sometimes when rookies pick up their first charged line, the force of the water tears the hose from their hands.

The water that comes out of the hose is called a fire stream. Firefighters

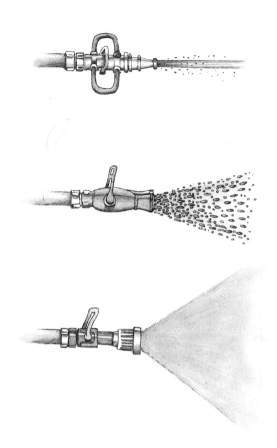

Hose nozzles of different shapes and sizes produce different kinds of fire streams. Solid streams of water (top) are used for reaching fires at a great distance; broken streams (middle) are for closer distances; and fog streams (bottom) are for saturating or cooling walls, ceilings, floors, and even furniture at close range.

Illustration copyright © 1998 by Scott Sroka

use different kinds of fire streams for fighting different kinds and sizes of fires. To get the fire stream they want, they use hoses and nozzles of different sizes and shapes, and change the pressure of the water. They follow a simple rule: "Small fire, small water; big fire, big water."

A "broken stream" nozzle causes the water to break into drops that sprinkle the fire like a heavy shower. If the firefighters were unable to get inside the house, they would attack the fire from a safe distance outside using a "solid stream" nozzle and a 2½-inch hose line. Each nozzleman on the charged hose lines opens the nozzle slightly to let the air out, then closes it. With the charged hose lines in hand, rescue teams can begin the primary search, and the ladder company can begin to ventilate the roof.

The primary search must be made quickly, since it is very hot, dark, and smoky in the house. Firefighters allow about fifteen minutes for the primary search. In many fires, the person reporting the fire tells the dispatcher that someone is still inside the building. At other fire scenes, firefighters may have to rely on other sources of information—neighbors, bystanders, or their own observations. For instance, an entrance ramp could indicate that a resident is in a wheelchair and will need special rescue procedures. Toys and bicycles in the yard are signs that children might be inside the home. Shirts and pants drying on an outside clothesline can help identify the size, age, and gender of the people who might be inside.

If a rescue team finds a door locked from the inside, they often use a special tool called a Halligan bar to pry the lock open and force their way inside. A Halligan bar is actually three tools in one—a claw, a lever, and a cutting blade. Rescue workers and ladder companies rely on the Halligan bar and the ax, known together as a "universal pack," to accomplish a great variety of jobs. Even if the smoke and fire have not reached the room they are searching, the firefighters keep on their SCBAs. They search in closets, under beds,

Firefighters search every corner of a building to find and rescue people who may be injured or trapped inside (opposite).

and behind tables, chairs, and shelves. As they move nearer the fire, the search becomes more difficult because the fire is dangerously hot and the smoke makes visibility poor. Remembering the rule "If you can't see your feet, get down on your knees," the firefighters drop to the floor where the air is cooler and less smoky. As they crawl from room to room, the firefighters constantly tap one hand on the boot of the firefighter in front so they don't get separated. If the person in front doesn't feel a tap, he stops, then crawls backward until he finds the firefighter behind him. They swing their ax handles in slow sweeping motions to feel under the furniture for a body. They search along the outside wall first, opening windows as they go to help ventilate the house. They have to be careful when they open windows, though; if too much heated gas has built up inside a room, letting in air can cause an explosion called a backdraft. Ventilating the roof helps prevent a backdraft by releasing the smoke and gas.

The searchers pause from time to time, listening for cries of help. After they search a room, they mark an X with chalk on the bottom of the door or put a chair in the doorway to show that the room has been searched. Once they find a person, one firefighter radios to the incident commander, then the incident commander radios the ambulance to bring a stretcher to the nearest entrance. The person is carried out while other firefighters drag the hose back outside, still on their hands and knees. The incident commander radios the dispatcher that the rescue has been completed. The ambulance company will begin treating the rescued victim for such problems as smoke inhalation, burns, and other injuries as they rush him to the hospital for full medical attention.

Firefighters always lead people out of burning buildings the safest way— by stairs, a fire escape, an outside ladder, or in the bucket of an aerial ladder. If necessary, they may be lowered by ropes or harnesses down the outside of

the building. Firefighters no longer have people jump out of burning buildings into life nets—too many people were hurt landing in the nets.

As the rescue teams search the house, the ladder company takes ladders,

Perched on their aerial ladder, firefighters cut holes in the roof with their axes and chain saws. Water is sprayed in the holes and trapped smoke, heat, and gases rise out.

Without a roof to stand on, firefighters attack the fire from aerial platforms and with remote-controlled nozzles.

axes, and chain saws off their truck. Usually two firefighters put an extension ladder against the house, then steady the ladder as two other firefighters climb it with one of the charged hose lines. With the blunt end of the ax they tap the roof to make sure it is safe to walk on. Carefully they hook a roof ladder over the peak of the roof above the room where light smoke is showing. Fire may already have burned up to this room from the living room. One firefighter stands at the bottom of the roof ladder with a charged hose line. The firefighter a few rungs above him pulls up some roof shingles with his ax, then starts his chain saw. An experienced firefighter can cut a four-foot-by-four-foot hole in the roof between the wooden support rafters in about one minute. Smoke wafts out of the hole, and the firefighters move quickly off the roof. When water is sprayed on the fire in the rooms directly under the roof, smoke, heat, and trapped gases will escape through the hole.

Roof ventilation is one of the most dangerous jobs, because the firefighters do not know how big the fire beneath them is. If they remove their masks in order to see more clearly, they are not protected if flames shoot out through the hole they have made. The roof may collapse, even though it seemed safe when they checked it. Companies equipped with an aerial ladder can avoid some of these dangers. Firefighters ride in a bucket or on a platform at the end of this ladder, which is mounted on the ladder truck. Its position is controlled by the truck driver.

Once the roof has been ventilated, firefighters ventilate the fire room from the outside by smashing the locked windows. With their charged attack lines, the engine teams enter the house, one close behind the other. They cannot see through the smoke, so the lead team locates the fire room by feeling for the doorjamb. They wait until they hear the sound of glass shattering. They aim the hose into the room, open the nozzle, then release a powerful stream of water. They move the stream in Z, O, and T patterns to soak the ceiling, walls, and floor around the fire. The smoke, heat, and gases escape through the windows. Another team of firefighters feels its way up the stairs and toward the room above the fire room. The burned floor could collapse, so they stay outside the door as they spray the room with a broken stream. The smoke and steam rise through the hole in the roof. In house fires like this one, firefighters need about a minute to extinguish, or "knock down," the fire. Then the firefighters follow their hose lines out of the house. The incident commander reports back to the dispatcher that the fire has been knocked down. Firefighters breathe a sigh of relief, but they know there is still a lot of work to be done before the fire is considered completely out. They wait for the incident commander to give them their next instructions.

Firefighter Safety

Avoiding chaos and confusion at the fire scene is the job of the incident commander, an experienced firefighter who plans the attack and commands the firefighters.

The incident commander is responsible for all the firefighters. He uses a "command assessment board" to help keep track of each one. Firefighters can get lost in a smoke-filled building or their SCBAs can run out of air. They may be overcome by smoke or trapped by falling debris. For safety they always try to work in pairs. Before entering or going behind a building or going up on a roof, the firefighters place one of two nametags on the command assessment board under their company name. They attach the other tag to their coat, helmet, or SCBA. When they return, they remove their tags from the board.

The dispatcher helps the incident commander keep track of the firefighters by radioing that he is "fifteen minutes into the incident" or "thirty minutes into the incident." This reminds the incident commander to look at the nametags and check if anyone is missing. If a firefighter doesn't pick up his nametag on time, a team is sent to search for him. Firefighters learn from the time they are rookies that their own safety and that of the other firefighters is of the greatest importance.

At a safe distance from the fire, a rescue vehicle or ambulance is set up as a rehabilitation, or "rehab," station. Most firefighters, no matter how physi-

Identification tags help the incident commander keep track of each firefighter at the scene. Incident commanders make sure firefighters take breaks regularly to avoid exhaustion.

During major fires, buses provide on-site headquarters for officers and equipment such as radios, computers, water supply maps, and building plans.

cally fit, can work for only fifteen to thirty minutes at a stretch when battling a serious fire. This is the usual limit of their air supply and also of their strength and stamina. Dizziness, nausea, dehydration, and fatigue are common side effects of firefighting and can lead to injuries and fatalities on the job. So after completing an assignment, such as rescuing a victim or cutting a hole in the roof, firefighters are required to go to rehab for medical evaluation, fluids, food, and rest. During this time they also refill their SCBAs. After about fifteen minutes of rest, most are ready for another assignment. Those whose blood pressure is too high or pulse too quick are held out until their vital signs return to normal. Seriously injured firefighters are sent in an ambulance to the nearest hospital. Because the work shifts are short, several companies are needed to fight a serious fire over several hours. The Ladies' Auxiliary or other volunteer organization serves juice, hot coffee, and meals to firefighters from a canteen—a bus, van, or truck equipped with a stove and a refrigerator.

Salvage and Overhaul

With pike poles and axes, the firefighters tear apart roofs (above, left) and take down walls (above, right) in search of hidden fires and embers that could reignite.

Once the fires have been knocked down and ventilation has cleared most of the smoke and heat from the house, crews from the rescue company, the ladder company, or both move back in to search again for possible victims. Even if everyone known to be inside is accounted for, there still may be someone in the building—perhaps a neighbor who entered the house to help out. During primary and secondary searches, firefighters always assume that someone could still be left inside.

The ladder company also continues to search for hidden fires or embers that could start a new fire. This process is called overhaul. With their turnout gear and SCBAs still on, firefighters take hooked poles, called pike poles, axes, and charged hose lines into the house. They tear down burned parts of walls and ceilings and pry up floors in the fire room and the room above. Any surface that feels warm to the touch is ripped open and sprayed with water. Firefighters also look for other signs of hidden fire, such as dried-out wallpaper or peeling paint.

Before leaving the fire scene, firefighters clean the mud, soot, and debris off their hoses, ladders, and other equipment.

The fire line keeps the public at a safe distance from the burning building and from the firefighters' trucks and equipment.

During and after the fire attack, firefighters try to salvage as much of the property in the house as possible. If there is time before water is sprayed on the fire, they remove furniture from a burning room to prevent it from being damaged by fire, smoke, and water. They also cover furniture below the fire area with large tarps to protect it from falling debris and water. After the fire is under control, the firefighters remove or cover furniture that might be sprayed with water during overhaul. The salvage team may haul burned sofas, bookshelves, and rugs out of the house and soak them with water. They may drag wet rugs outside to dry, sweep up broken glass and other debris, pump water out of a basement, and cover broken windows with plywood or heavy plastic.

During salvage and overhaul, firefighters try to discover where and how the fire started. They look at the smoke patterns on the walls and ceilings to see how the fire moved through the house. Sometimes they look at light bulbs. After ten minutes of 1,000-degree heat, a light bulb will point toward the source of the greatest heat. The firefighters are careful to save all possible evidence until the incident commander, fire marshal, or fire investigator has a chance to look at it. They may take photographs of burned walls, collect pieces of wood, or look for footprints and other evidence if they suspect that someone started the fire on purpose.

Once the house has been completely overhauled, the incident commander radios the dispatcher that all companies are preparing to leave the scene. If the hoses, equipment, and tools are covered in mud, soot, or debris, the firefighters give them a light washing before loading them onto the trucks. The trucks and equipment are not perfectly clean, but they are in good enough condition to respond to another call if necessary. Several hours after the call came in, the firefighters return to the station.

Back at the Station

Back at the station, the firefighters park their vehicles in the garage. As they take off their turnout gear, they may be greeted by those firefighters who missed the call but waited at the station in case extra manpower was needed.

At a paid station, the firefighters on duty may clean the equipment, take a shower, have something to eat, or get some rest or sleep until the next call

After a fire, firefighters give their trucks a thorough cleaning—inside and out—to keep them in perfect working order.

Hoses used at the fire are inspected, repaired, cleaned thoroughly, then hung to dry (above). Dry hoses are folded or rolled carefully before they are loaded back onto the pumper trucks (above, right). Tools are returned to their proper places on the trucks (opposite). At the scene of a fire, no time can be wasted looking for misplaced tools.

comes in. At volunteer stations, the firefighters might hang up their turnout gear and go home to rest. Or they might take a shower, get dressed, and go on to their regular paying jobs. If they are not too exhausted, they take some time to clean the equipment with the firefighters who didn't make the truck.

First they unload the hose and replace it with clean hose. Members of the engine company stretch out the sections of hose and clean them thoroughly with soap and water, and sometimes a scrub brush or broom, to remove all soot, oil, and mud. They check the couplings for damage, then hang the hoses to dry in the hose tower or lay them on flat drying racks. After a day or two, the dry hoses are rolled or folded in a variety of ways, depending on the size and use of the hose. The doughnut roll and twin doughnut roll, for instance, are open circles and are used when firefighters need to carry fifty-foot-long sections of attack hose over their shoulders. The horseshoe load

Turnout gear is cleaned, repaired, and hung in the garage, ready to be grabbed at the next call.

and accordion load are patterns used for loading attack or supply hose into the hose compartment on the fire engine. Correct loading keeps the hose from getting kinks or knots when it is unrolled or unfolded at the fire.

The firefighters clean soot from their coats, pants, boots, helmets, and facepieces and refill their SCBA tanks. They clean and repair damaged tools and load them back on the vehicles. All vehicles are thoroughly washed with soap and water, then dried and polished. The firefighters check sirens, lights, ignition, tires, fuel, and oil.

Firefighters keep their vehicles completely clean and in perfect working order. Some firefighters say that the vehicles' condition shows how good the fire department is. Taking care of the expensive ladder trucks and engines also keeps them in working order for many years. A new engine costs about $500,000 and a new ladder truck about $850,000. These vehicles usually last about fifteen years, but some thirty- and forty-year-old trucks are still used every day. One fire department in Los Angeles uses a seventy-year-old fireboat as well as a new computerized boat. Most departments upgrade their older ladder trucks and engines part by part before replacing the whole vehicle.

Life at the Firehouse

For many firefighters, the station is a "home away from home" when they are on duty. Dormitory bedrooms provide a place to stay rested (left), and exercise rooms (above) provide a place to stay in shape.

When not hard at work, firefighters may spend some time relaxing in the station's recreation room, which is usually furnished with sofas, comfortable chairs, bookshelves, a television, and a VCR. The walls are often decorated with photographs of the companies and the fires they have fought, as well as trophies and awards the firefighters have received for bravery and community service. The recreation room is used for special events and holiday parties that include family and friends.

When paid firefighters are on duty, they rest and sleep at the station.

Inside the Firehouse

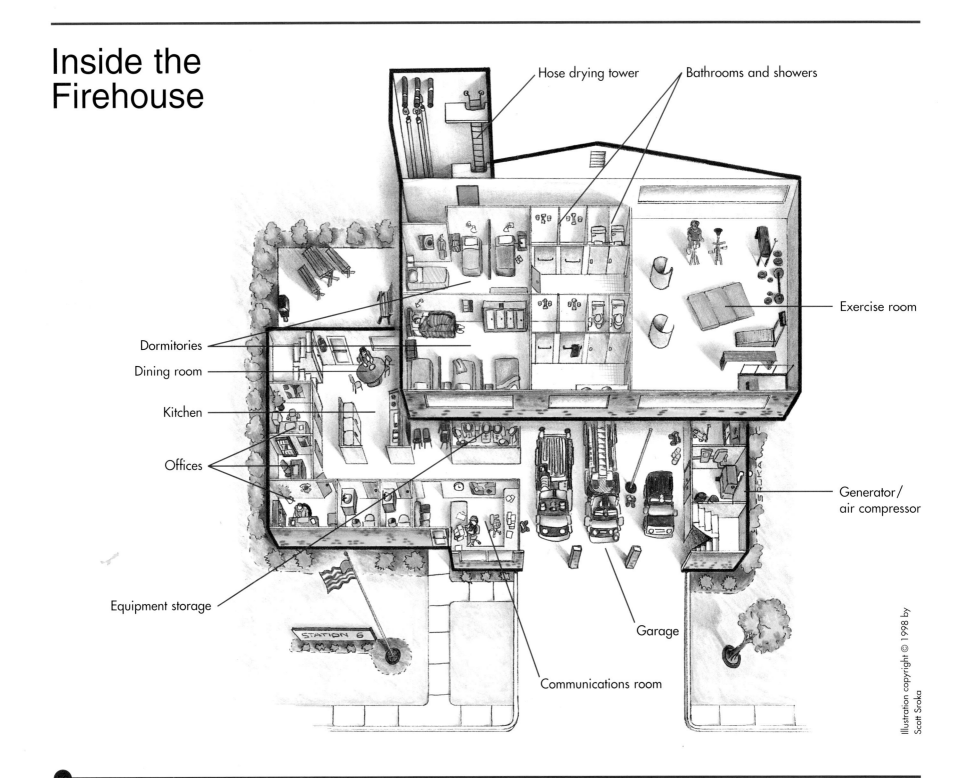

Hose drying tower

Bathrooms and showers

Exercise room

Dormitories

Dining room

Kitchen

Offices

Generator/
air compressor

Equipment storage

STATION 6

Garage

Communications room

Illustration copyright © 1998 by
Scott Sroka

Volunteers may stay there if they are too tired to drive home after fighting a fire. Firefighters sleep in dormitories that contain bunk beds, cots, or even Murphy beds, which fold up into the wall when not being used. If a station has both men and women firefighters, they may have separate dormitories or they may use folding screens for privacy. Some firefighters bring their own pillows, blankets, bedspreads, and even stuffed animals given to them by their children. Instead of closets, fire stations usually have a locker room where firefighters store their clothes and personal belongings.

Getting from their beds to the trucks quickly has always been a challenge for firefighters, especially in two- or three-story stations. In 1878, during the era of horse-drawn fire engines, when firefighters slept upstairs to avoid the smells from the horse stalls on the first floor, the sliding pole was introduced. The sliding pole was considered a great timesaver at first, but too many firefighters suffered broken or sprained ankles when using them. Most stations today have stairs, and firefighters say they can get down the stairs as quickly as down a pole, and more safely. Now firefighters sleep above the trucks, but in the few stations that have sliding poles, special doors help prevent the exhaust fumes from rising through the opening. Foam padding at the bottom of the pole keeps firefighters from being injured.

When the alarm sounds—or when the dinner bell rings—firefighters rush downstairs. The kitchen is usually combined with an eating area that can seat all the firefighters on duty, and a few extras. The kitchen may have two or three refrigerators, one for each shift, so that groceries don't get mixed up. Firefighters usually fix themselves breakfast and eat take-out food or sandwiches for lunch, but they cook and eat dinner together. They split up the responsibilities of choosing a recipe, making a grocery list, shopping, cooking, cleaning up, and collecting grocery money. When they go shopping, they always take their turnout gear and trucks, so they can respond to

Firefighters take turns shopping for groceries used in preparing their meals at the station.

Fire station kitchens are often large and equipped for cooking meals for dozens of hungry firefighters.

The most popular meals at the fire station are those that can be prepared quickly and reheated easily because dinners may be interrupted at any moment by a fire call.

a call without having to go back to the station. Firefighters on duty are never separated from their trucks and turnout gear.

Most firehouse dinners are simple and quickly prepared: pasta, stew, hamburgers on the grill. At some stations, firefighters from different ethnic backgrounds share the cooking of their cultures. The style of cooking and the traditions surrounding meals vary from station to station.

One firefighter in Florida brings in home-smoked mullet to share with the other firefighters. They often joke that he has nearly burned down his own house smoking those fish. A retired volunteer firefighter at that station has been bringing in doughnuts every Sunday morning for twenty-five years. He sits around the kitchen table with the other firefighters to enjoy breakfast and tales from the field.

Firefighters gather around the dining table for meals but use the confer-

In the fire station's conference room, the incident commander and the firefighters gather to discuss what happened at previous fires. Each firefighter contributes to the discussion so they can all learn from one another.

ence room for more serious meetings. After each fire, the incident commander and the firefighters who responded to the call sit down at a large table in the conference room for a critique and discussion of the fire. Because the fire scene is chaotic and firefighters can't always see or understand what the others are doing, the critique allows them to learn the complete story of a fire or emergency.

On a blackboard, the incident commander diagrams the burning building, the streets around it, neighboring buildings, and the positions of the ladder truck, the engines and hose lines, rescue squad, and ambulance. Officers take turns explaining what their companies did at the fire. Other firefighters also speak up, adding their own details. As they talk, the incident

In the fire station office, firefighters write reports of each fire and emergency call they handle and take care of company business.

commander fills in the drawing, showing where the ladders were placed, where the roof was ventilated, where the victim was found, and where fire was discovered during overhaul. The incident commander may ask the officers questions: Why did the engine company use one supply line instead of two? Why did the ladder company place their ladder in front of a door? Why didn't one rescue company go through rehab after the primary search? The discussion helps the firefighters see what they did right and wrong. Rookies and experienced firefighters alike learn from these critiques.

"Every fire is different," says Lieutenant Mike Garcia, who has been a career firefighter in one county in Virginia for thirteen years while volunteering in another for fifteen years. "You always have those times when you come back from a fire saying, 'I've never seen that before.'"

"Sometimes you go into the critique knowing you made some mistakes," says another firefighter. "After an hour or so of talking about it, you learn why you made the mistakes. And you learn how to prevent them next time. Other times you think you did everything right, then you find out you could have done a much better job. You might get your feelings hurt, but you come out confident that you can do your job even better. It's a good feeling."

Fire Prevention and Safety

Firefighters sometimes visit schools (left) to teach students about fire prevention and safety. Fire inspectors visit public buildings (above) to make sure that fire alarms, smoke detectors, and sprinklers work properly.

Every year, fires kill about 4,500 people in the United States and injure about 133,000 more. Fires destroy more than $9 billion worth of property. In addition to fighting fires, fire departments try to prevent them by inspecting public buildings and encouraging people to install fire extinguishers and smoke detectors in their homes. They also visit schools to teach about firefighting equipment and fire prevention and to let the students see what a firefighter in full turnout gear looks like. Young children who are caught in fires sometimes run away from the rescue teams trying to save them, frightened by the sight of a firefighter in big boots, a hood, and a face mask, with a hissing SCBA.

Alarms placed inside buildings can be pulled to warn people to get out. Public pay phones located outside the building can be used without a coin to dial 911.

Firefighters say everyone should know certain rules about fire safety and prevention.

IF YOU ARE IN A BUILDING THAT CATCHES FIRE:
- Leave the building immediately.
- Don't go back for any reason.
- If you are in bed, roll out onto the floor.
- Crawl to the door and feel it with the back of your hand.
- If the door is hot, try to escape through a window.
- If the door is not hot, crawl out the door.
- Close the door behind you to slow down the spread of smoke and fire.
- In a smoky room or hallway, crawl. The air is cleanest near the floor.
- Go to another building or house and dial 911 or the number of your local fire station, or pull the handle on a fire alarm box in the building or on the street.

IF YOUR CLOTHES CATCH FIRE:

- **STOP** right where you are. Don't panic or run.
- **DROP** to the ground and cover your face with your hands.
- **ROLL** over and over to put out the flames.

Fire safety at home should include a fire escape plan (above). Portable ladders (right) are recommended for upper-story bedrooms.

PLAN AHEAD FOR SAFETY:

- Never use matches or lighters unless an adult is with you.
- Suggest to your parents that they put fire extinguishers and smoke detectors in your house.
- Make an escape plan with your family. Try to have two escape routes from each room.
- Practice your escape plan at least twice a year in the dark. Pick a place away from the house for your family to meet, such as your mailbox or the nearest neighbor's house.

Every home should be equipped with smoke detectors that are checked regularly.